The Let's Talk Library™

Let's Talk About When Someone You Love Is in the Hospital

Marianne Johnston

The Rosen Publishing Group's
PowerKids Press™
New York

Special thanks to Parkridge Hospital in Rochester, New York, for help in acquiring photographs.

Published in 1997 by The Rosen Publishing Group, Inc.
29 East 21st Street, New York, NY 10010

First Edition

Book Design: Erin McKenna

Photo Illustrations: Cover, pp. 8, 11, 12, 15, 16, 20 by Carrie Ann Grippo; pp. 4, 7, 19 by Seth Dinnerman.

Johnston, Marianne.
    Let's talk about when someone you love is in the hospital / Marianne Johnston.
       p.   cm. — (The let's talk library)
    Includes index.
    Summary: Discusses visiting loved ones in the hospital, how to make them feel better, how they look as patients, and the scary feeling one has at such a time.
    ISBN 0-8239-5037-9
    1. Hospitals—Juvenile literature. 2. Hospital care—Juvenile literature. 3. Children—Preparation for medical care—Juvenile literature. [1. Hospitals.] I. Title. II. Series.
    RA963.5.J643 1996
    362.1'1—dc20
                                      96-41652
                                         CIP
                                       AC

Manufactured in the United States of America

Table of Contents

Laurie's Mom

Laurie's mom became really sick one day. Laurie's dad took Mom to the **hospital** (HOS-pih-tul). The doctors there said she had to stay for a while. Laurie was worried. She missed her mom. And Dad was tired from working, cooking, cleaning, and visiting Mom. Laurie told her dad that she missed Mom. Her dad hugged her and said that he missed Mom, too. But the hospital was the best place for Mom right now. And she would be home soon. Then Laurie felt better. But she couldn't wait until Mom was home again.

◀ It can be a sad, scary time when someone in your family is in the hospital. It helps to talk about it.

5

Someone You Love Is Sick

It can be scary when someone you love is sick enough to go to the hospital. Things at home can change a lot. You may have to help out by folding laundry, making your bed, or setting the table. You may miss the person who is in the hospital. But if someone is really sick, the hospital is a good place for him or her to be. There are doctors and nurses who can take care of a sick person all day and night. They can help that person get well. Then that person can come home.

Talking about why someone needs to be in the hospital can help you feel better. ▶

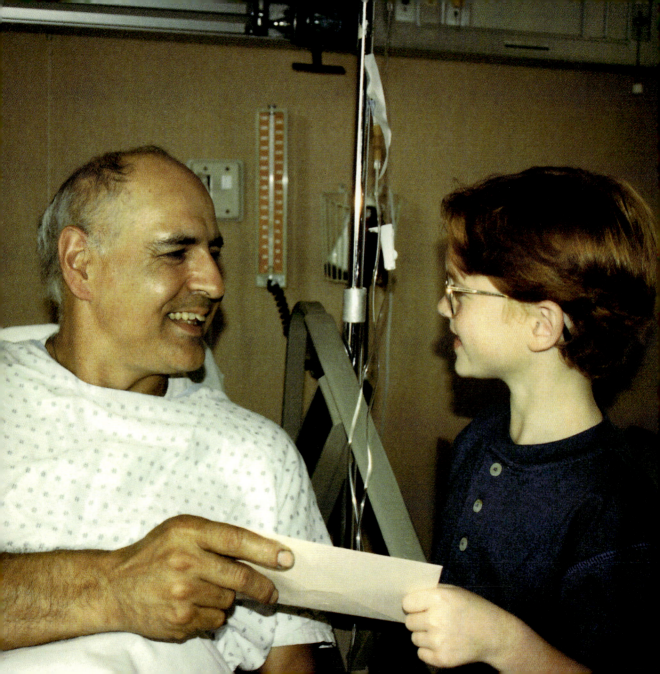

Visiting at the Hospital

One of the best things you can do for someone who is in the hospital is to visit him. If you were sick and away from home, you would want your family and friends to visit you. Having **visitors** (VIZ-ih-terz) lets the sick person know that people care about him. You might be nervous about going to the hospital. Or you may not want to go at all. It's okay to be nervous or scared. Just remember that a visit from you will help make the sick person feel a lot better.

◀ Visiting someone in the hospital
can cheer him up.

Rules for Visiting

Once a person is admitted into a hospital, he is called a **patient** (PAY-shunt). Patients need lots of rest. That can be hard to get if they have visitors all the time. So the visitors can only come at certain times of the day. These are called visiting hours. Visiting hours are usually during the morning and the evening.

Patients like visitors, but they need quiet time too. ▶

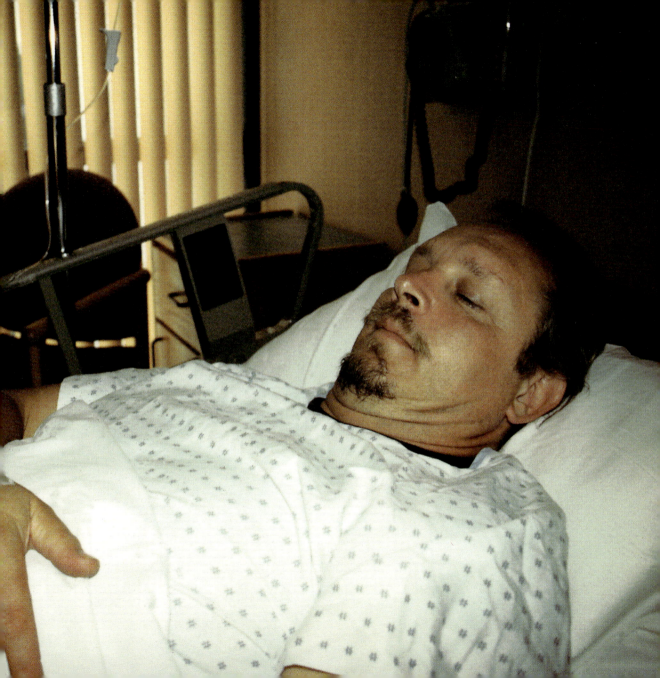

EMERGENCY
PARKING FOR:
EMERGENCY
NURSING HOME
OUTPATIENT SERVICES
ADMITTING AND
DISCHARGE

Hospitals Can Be Scary

A hospital is a busy place. Nurses and doctors and other hospital workers always seem to be in a hurry. Sometimes hospitals smell strange, like a bathroom just after it's been cleaned.

The hospital may be a little scary at first. But there are lots of people who can help you find your way around. The hospital is a safe, good place. The people there are helping someone you love get better.

◀ There are signs inside and outside the hospital that will show you where to go.

13

You Look Funny

When people are sick, they don't look like they normally do. Your grandma may look too thin. Your dad's skin may seem to be a slightly different color. This is because he is very sick. Once he is well, he'll look like he used to.

Some kinds of medicine make people feel tired or act differently. Your dad may be too tired to talk to you. But he's very happy you're there to see him.

14

The person you visit may look a little different, ▶
but he is still the same person who loves you.

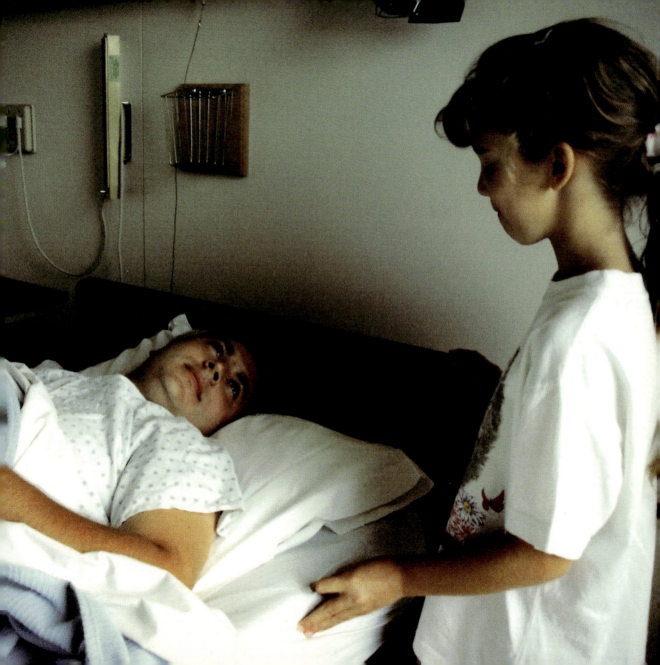

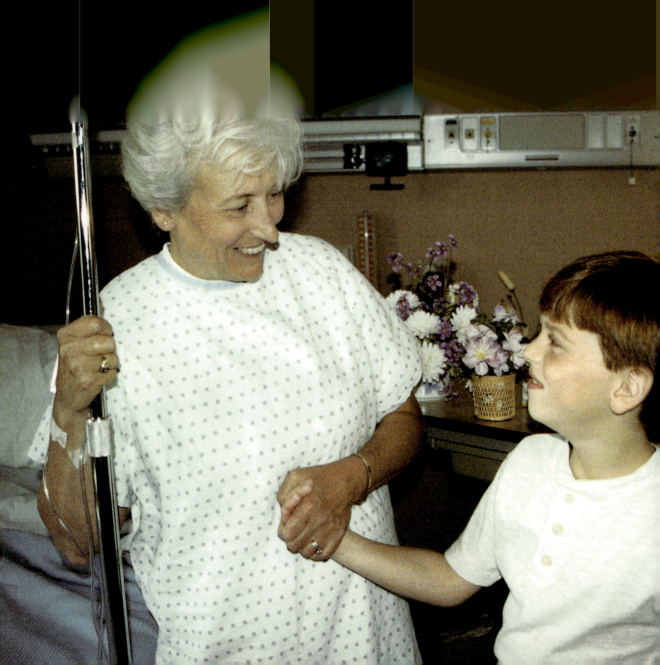

Tubes and Machines

Sometimes patients in hospitals are hooked up to tubes or machines. This can look scary. But the tubes and machines help that person get better. Most patients have an IV drip. This is a tube hooked up on one end to a bag of water and sugar, which is food for that person's body. On the other end is a needle that is placed in a **vein** (VAYN) in the person's arm. The patient may also be hooked up to a **monitor** (MON-ih-ter). Doctors use this machine to make sure the person's heart is beating the way it should.

◀ A patient who has an IV can still get out of bed and walk around.

It's Okay to Ask

You will see many things in the hospital that you don't understand. Don't be afraid to ask questions about them. If you want to know what a certain machine does, ask someone about it. If you're wondering what's making the person you love sick, ask your parent or the doctor or nurse. You can even ask the patient. New things seem less scary as you learn more about them.

A doctor or nurse may be able to answer some of your questions. ▶

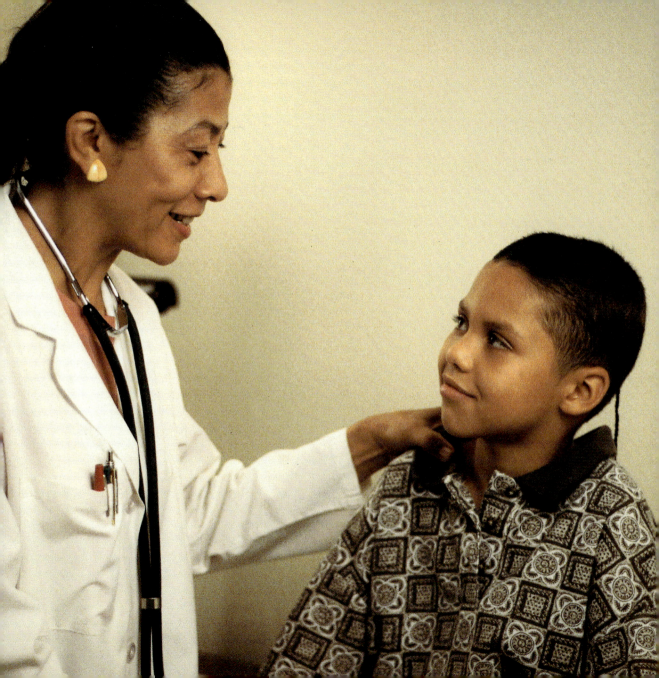

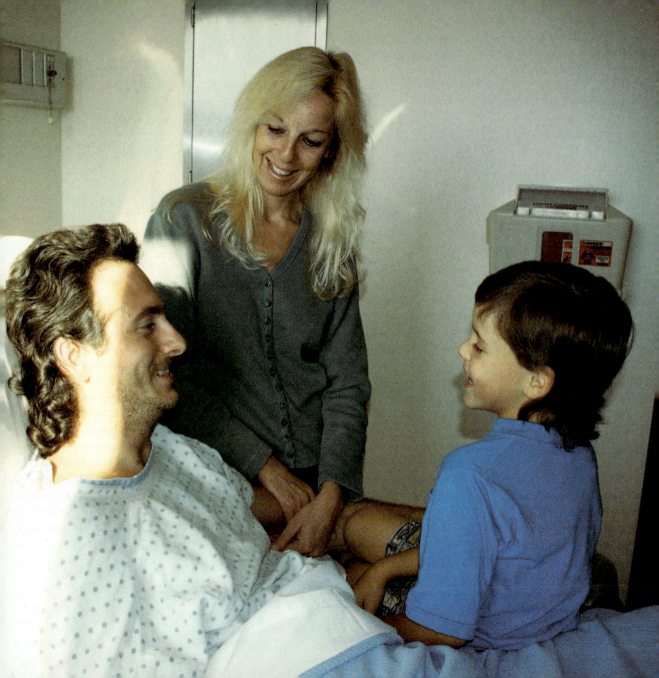

It's Okay to Talk

When someone is sick, it is a hard time for everyone. It helps to talk about what's going on. It's okay to ask the patient how he or she is feeling. Some people think that they should pretend that everything is okay. This doesn't help at all. It doesn't make the sickness go away. And it doesn't make the patient feel better. The patient may want to talk about his illness. So don't be afraid to show your **concern** (kon-SERN). It will help everyone feel better.

◀ Don't be afraid to ask the patient how he is feeling. It will help him feel better to know that you care.

21

Brighten the Room

Visiting a patient in the hospital can make both of you feel better. You can also make a special card. The message can say that you hope the person gets well soon. A bright, cheerful card can make the hospital room look more fun. It will also remind the patient of you after you leave. Some people bring flowers. Whether you bring something or just visit, it will help cheer up the patient. It will also remind that person of all the people who love her, and help her think about getting better.

Glossary

concern (kon-SERN) Interest; worry.

hospital (HOS-pih-tul) A place for the care of people who are sick or hurt.

monitor (MON-ih-ter) A machine that is used to check or control something.

patient (PAY-shunt) A person who is being treated by a doctor.

vein (VAYN) A tube in your body that blood flows through.

visitor (VIZ-ih-ter) A person who goes to see someone else.

Index